Walks from Your Car

Blackburn and Bolton

by
Ron and Marlene Freethy

Dalesman Books
1991

The Dalesman Publishing Company Ltd.,
Clapham via Lancaster, LA2 8EB

First published 1991

Printed by Peter Fretwell & Sons Ltd.,
Goulbourne Street, Keighley, West Yorkshire BD21 1PZ

Contents

Cover design by Barbara Yates

Introduction

MANY of these walks would not have been possible a few years ago. Everyone seemed to accept that Lancashire made brass, created muck and pollution and anyone who walked around such ugly spots as Blackburn, Bolton and Darwen must be in need of psychiatric treatment. Such an idea was wrong then and it is even more wrong today.

The West Pennine Moors now has a developing ranger service, an amazingly comprehensive selection of well marked footpaths and an increasing number of Information Centres with facilities for children and the disabled. The area may have come late into the tourist market but it is catching up quickly.

It is hard to imagine that some of the walks covered in this book are over moors once polluted by run off from lead mines, pock marked with coal mines, smothered under blankets of natural fog and man made smog from the mills and bleach works. Only the natural fog remains and back has come the beauty to the Pennine valleys.

No wonder there was an outcry when, in 1990, planners from south of the Wash proposed to swamp the area beneath 200 square miles of alien conifers which in time could be harvested for a profit.

Following an outcry this idea was dropped — some would say shelved. Those of us who walk these uplands need to keep a wary eye open to ensure such ill-advised schemes stay in a Whitehall desk and gather dust.

Darwen Moor, Jubilee Tower and Sunnyhurst Wood

Parking: From the Blackburn to Darwen road (A666) a right turn indicates Sunnyhurst Wood. Pass the signs to the park and Information Centre and continue to climb until The Sunnyhurst Hotel is reached. Continue beyond the hotel and find a car park on the right. The circular walk is based from this park.

LEAVING the car park, turn right and at a junction of three paths follow the left route, which is a metalled road from which there are splendid views of Blackburn and Darwen down to the left. A tower comes into view on the right as the path approaches the wall of Sunnyhurst Hey Reservoir. At first sight the metalled path seems to end at the reservoir but the route bears left across a field to a stile leading into a disused quarry. Turn right through the quarry in which grows heather and bilberry and then climb a steep incline and through a gate. There are a number of seats here and along most of the rest of the route — all ideal places for a picnic.

The stony path climbs very steeply and can be quite tricky especially after rain. At the point where the path forks take the right hand path, but spare time to look over the stone wall to the left. Here is a splendid view of Darwen, with the tall chimney of India mill especially prominent. This was built of handmade bricks in the style of the Campanile in St. Mark's Square in Venice. The old Lancashire Mill owners worshipped profits but many were also men of taste and it showed in the design of the industrial buildings which they commissioned.

The Jubilee Tower was so named because it was constructed in 1898 to celebrate the Silver Jubilee of Victoria's coronation in 1838 — she ascended the throne in 1837. These moors are usually breezy and the wind gets stronger as the stone steps to the top of the tower are climbed. This tower stands on top of the 372 metres (1225 feet) hill and on the top storey are indicators pointing out the highland areas which can be seen on a clear day. The list is, to say the least, impressive and includes Pendle, Great Whernside, Fountains Fell, Fairsnape Fell, Langdale Pikes, Bowfell, Coniston Old Man, Kinder Scout, Holcolm Fell, Boulsworth, Black Combe, Snaefell on the Isle of Man and Snowdon plus other Welsh Mountains.

From the tower the path winds gently downhill with Sunnyhurst

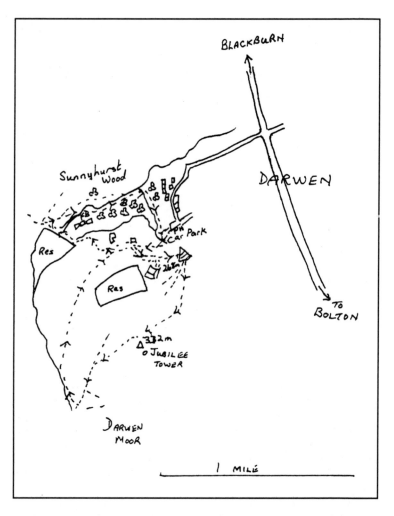

Hey Reservoir down to the right and regular seats set into the heather on the left. Approach a neat little wood down in a dip of a hill to the right. Just beyond a seat at the right angled corner of the path turn right over an unmarked stile. The route then descends steeply and during wet weather rather dangerously towards an obvious path. Turn right along a metalled track and head towards Barnsdale Reservoir keeping one of its feeder streams, called Stepback Brook, on the left.

Pass through two gates, alongside a farm on the right and then a bailiff's caravan and anglers' car park. A not very obvious footpath now forks left off the metalled track down through a rough field and meets a road heading towards the nearby Earnsdale Reservoir which faces the walker. Those who are tired at this point could continue straight along the track to the car park, but those with enough energy can continue and complete the circuit by strolling through Sunnyhurst wood. Near the reservoir is a cattle grid and a gate. Pass through the gate and bear right following the line of a thick hawthorn hedge. Ignore the right fork but follow the left fork which passes across the front of the reservoir. About half way across this causeway is the old boundary stone between Darwen and Tockholes. Behind is an excellent view of the tower perched and looking like a space rocket on Darwen moor.

At the end of the causeway turn right through a "kissing gate" into Sunnyhurst wood. A network of paths runs through the wood, but we prefer to bear to the right all the time. Find a footbridge down to the right which crosses the river and then climbs before descending to a dell dominated by the temple-like structure bearing a crude inscription "The Gift of Charles Spencer Greenway August 10th 1912".

From this point the main path continues into the more organised public park with bridges over the river Darwen, an information centre and a cafe. Our route swings right from the main path and climbs steeply to the car park close to the Sunnyhurst hotel. It is worth stopping frequently, not only to get your breath back, but to watch the rich variety of bird life including jays, great spotted woodpeckers, treecreepers and the local woodpigeons. Few walks can offer such a variety of habitats as this one which is so close to the industrial town of Darwen.

Around Haslingden Grane Reservoirs

Parking: From Haslingden follow the Grane road (B6232) which leads to Blackburn (south) and Darwen. Pass the signs to Helmshore Museum. On the left is the Duke of Wellington hotel and beyond this on the right is Clough Head Information Centre. There is a picnic site and toilet facilities.

FROM the Information Centre follow the yellow marker signs, cross the Grane road and head for the dam of Calf Hey reservoir but remember that Haslingden Grane was made up of a number of small settlements. Indeed Calf Hey means the area where cows were retained within a hedge (once called a hey). It is still possible to see the remains of Rothwell Fold but much of this is now beneath the waters. There is a trough here which provided the villagers with water before the reservoir was constructed. Its job was to filter out pebbles and grit before the water was culverted towards the houses. There was also a Methodist chapel hereabouts and although the building has gone the inscribed gravestones remain. The car park is actually built on the site of Chapel Row, a group of stone cottages once part of Grane village.

Continue to follow the path along the top of the dam and look down left towards Ogden reservoir and right along the waters of Calf Hey. Calf Hey was constructed between 1854 and 1859 to supply Bury and Radcliffe whilst Ogden was built in 1912 to supply the towns developing along the Irwell valley. It was at this time that the area was deliberately depopulated because it was thought that the people would pollute the water. A much more realistic attitude prevails these days and such compulsory movements would not be allowed.

Bear right at the end of the track and follow the bank until the path forks. Take the left fork towards Hog Low Clough. Rainfall up here can be violent and to prevent stone and silt being flushed into the reservoir a series of stilling ponds have been constructed to allow these to settle out. There is also a system to allow the water to be diverted into either Calf Hey or Ogden lower down the valley depending upon demand. There is also a good selection of trees here which allows bird life to increase in numbers and variety. Redstart, jay and great spotted woodpecker are now regularly recorded here.

There is a circular route around the reservoir but where it meets the Rossendale Way turn left around a belt of trees to the right and

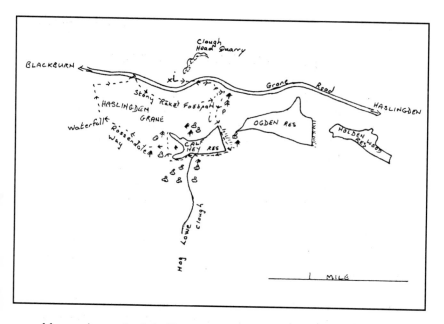

old quarries to the left. Turn right along a wide track which heads towards the Grane road. The Rossendale Way then reaches the Grane Road. Swing right just before the road and follow Stony Rake footpath back to the starting point. Spend some time looking around the ruins of cottages, once the homes of hand loom weavers. Stony Rake was once the route taken by pack horses through the valley in the days before the turnpike road (now the Grane Road).

An Afterthought

FOR those who want to see living history it is but a short distance on the Haslingden road to the Helmshore Textile Museum which is well signed. There is a car park, cafe, shop and many exhibits tracing the history of textile production. Here we can put some meat on the bones seen during the walk. There is also a short riverside walk and a super example of a waterwheel. Inside (there is an entrance fee) are spinning mules, Hargreaves's Spinning Jenny, Arkwright's Water Frame and some handlooms typical of the type used in the cottages of Haslingden Grane.

Upper Haslingden Grane

Parking: Clough Head Quarry car park is used as for walk No. 2. With careful planning it is possible to enjoy this area without having a car. At weekends the East Lancashire railway runs steam trains out of Bury to Ramsbottom. From the station there is a bus service to Haslingden Grane. In the early 19th century there was a population of around 3,000 with all the essential services such as a shop, pub, chapel, church (dedicated to St. Stephen) and a simple school. There was, apparently many an illicit whisky still and this they made from "grane" and thus earned their name. Following the reservoir construction the three mills closed and folk left the area. In 1926 St. Stephen's church was demolished and rebuilt further down the valley. With the West Pennine valleys attracting more and more tourists a great deal of life is returning to the Grane.

FROM the Quarry car park find a footpath up to the left. Follow this to a junction with a wider track which is a section of the increasingly popular Rossendale Way. turn right.

Pass the disused quarry at Deep Clough. Quarrying in the 19th century was an essential and therefore profitable industry. The tough millstone grit was needed to build the increasing number of mills and houses for the workers, but especially the larger mansions of the businessmen. The towns also needed paving stone and smaller cobbles or setts for the roads. One of our grandparents came to Lancashire as a "setter".

After the quarry the route goes on to Windy Harbour farm and from here the track is followed down to its union with the Grane road. Cross this and up to the right is the Duke of Wellington Hotel which provides a variety of bar snacks and is popular with walkers in the summer due in no small measure to its children's playground. The views along the string of reservoirs give the place a continental feeling which is reinforced by the good fresh healthy breeze which during a hot July day is most welcome. It is not so welcome in January but the hot soup compensates for this.

After the diversion get your wellington boots moving again returning to the track to Windy Harbour farm. Take the path on the opposite side which passes between Holden Wood reservoir on the left and Ogden reservoir on the right. After this turn right alongside Ogden reservoir keeping the water on the right.

This is once more an ideal stretch of the walk for those interested

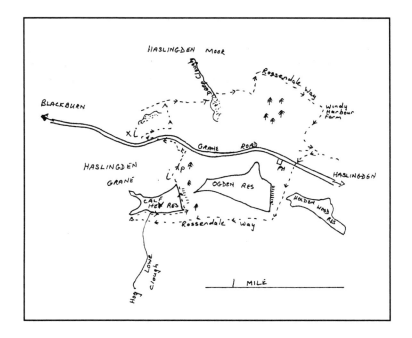

in bird watching. Herons are regular visitors to the shallows whilst out in the middle wildfowl find good feeding and roosting. Two species which are frequently seen include the black and white tufted ducks and the pochards which have red heads and grey bodies. These descriptions only fit the males, the females are much duller. This makes sense as it is only the ducks which incubate the eggs, and the males would be conspicuous to predators if they sat on the nest.

Common sandpipers are also a feature in this area during the summer whilst in winter fieldfares and redwings feed on the hawthorn berries and kestrels are residents feeding on small mammals and breeding among the piles of stones from the crumbling disused houses and in the quarries which are typical of the Grane.

The area is also of interest to botanists who wish to know more about moorland grasses and sedges. Here grow mat-grass, sheeps fescue, bent, sedge and both the soft and bog rush. In the early days the Graners used to collect the rushes and peel back the stem to reveal a soft interior. This was soaked in mutton fat and thus they had rush lights to illuminate their meagre homes.

This area can be bleak indeed during the winter and in snow the Grane road is usually the first of the local routes to close.

This route, however, is a fine cold weather walk especially after light snow or frost which brings out the sharp features of the landscape.

Continue onwards, if you can tear yourself away from watching the wildfowl. At Calf Hey reservoir turn right over the dam. Pass an Information Board and then follow the obvious path back to the car park.

Jumbles Reservoir and Country Park near Bolton

Parking: This circular walk can be based either at Ousels Nest (ousel is the old English name for a blackbird) car park — there is an excellent picnic site here but no toilets — or from the Waterfold car park near the Information Centre and toilets. In the summer 1991 a much larger Information Centre, bookshop and cafe are to be provided. The opening times of the Information Centre are as follows:-

Easter to October	*Wednesday and Saturdays*	*1.00pm to 5pm*
	Sunday	*11.00am to 6pm*
Bank Holiday		*10.00am to 6pm*
In winter	*Sunday*	*10.00am to 5pm*

Local artefacts and natural history exhibits are on display and a selection of books and leaflets is available.

Ousels Nest car park is signed from the Chapeltown road between Bromley Cross and Turton. Waterfold Car Park is signed from Bradshaw Road the A676 from Bolton to Ramsbottom.

THE PATH from Ousels Nest car park descends steeply cutting between a thick hedgerow which is a delight to naturalists, and a number of neat bungalows. The route crosses beneath the railway line and the right after crossing a field. A short distance along a wide track (suitable for residents' cars and those on their way to the Civil Service Sailing Club), Jumbles reservoir is then signed left, and descends over rough fields fringed by trees — all excellent bird watching country.

Bradshaw Brook once flowed through a valley on the sides of which were farms and weavers' cottages. As the industrial revolution gathered pace, Horrobin mill developed from a farm based fulling mill but by 1780 it had become a bleachworks which did not close until 1941. Industry and better housing demanded more and more water and Jumbles is the most recent and most southerly of three reservoirs in Bradshaw Brook, the others being Wayoh and Entwistle. Jumbles only opened in 1971 and provides 10 million gallons of compensation water for the Croal-Irwell system each day. It does not, however, provide drinking water and as such has been ideal to develop into a country park with boating, angling and natural history.

The path climbs steeply, but wooden steps have been set in the

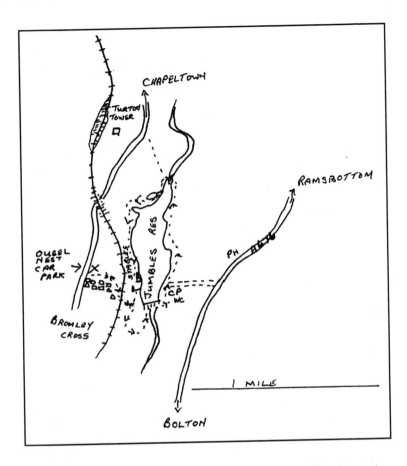

bank and soon Waterfold car park is reached. From the Information Centre the path descends towards a bay, overlooked by seats which are ideal for a picnic, and which is very popular with anglers. This area used to be the lodge of the drowned Horrobin mill and close by is a nature conservation area, access to which is sensibly restricted. Just to the right of the path almost hidden by vegetation is a loading ramp constructed of stone and also associated with the mill. Beyond this a flight of steps leads up to a pond rich in wildlife which was another of the lodges of Horrobin mill and because of its shape the locals call it "Coffin Lodge".

The route turns left over a bridge with views of the reservoir to the left and an extensive disused quarry to the right with Bradshaw Brook passing beneath. Pass Lees cottages which were the mill workers' dwellings and then negotiate a stile close to yet another mill lodge. Continue on an obvious route past the sailing club on the left and strike through Horrobin Fold in which the horses used by the mill to transport their goods were stabled. The area is now used as a pony trekking centre. Beyond this a right turn leads across a field to the track back up to Ousel Nest car park.

Around Peel Tower at Holcombe

Parking: Holcombe Moor car park and picnic site is on the right and reached from the Holcombe Brook to Haslingden road — the B6214. This leads to the A676 Bolton road. Like many other parts of industrial Lancashire there are more and more car parks and picnic sites being l.aid out. It seems that the more walkers are out and about, the more walks are provided. Let us hope this attitude continues.

AT the car park look at the informative map of the West Pennine Moors before crossing the road and through a stile. This crosses a field and then meets a cobbled bridleway leading up from Holcombe Brook. Turn right towards a small group of cottages but sweeping left just before reaching them. The recently renovated footpath zig-zags its way upwards towards the Peel Tower. Before this, however, pass Top O'th Moor Farm and beyond this are panoramic views down into the Irwell valley and across to the urban sprawl of Bury and Manchester.

Just below is the mosque of the Islamic college and beyond this on summer weekends often comes a wisp of steam from the East Lancashire Railway.

This is best known as the Red Rose Line and the "Irwell Express" between Bury and Rawtenstall is becoming an increasingly popular tourist attraction. We sometimes enjoy following the route taken by the Victorian mill workers from Bury and in those days the line actually reached Bacup. They alighted at Ramsbottom and walked up to Holcombe Brook and then they enjoyed a day on the moor.

From Top O'th Moor farm the footpath soon climbs over the peaty uplands to the Peel Tower which dominates the landscape for miles around. So it should since it is a 112 feet high (34 metres) tower of millstone grit perched on top of a moorland which is 1126 feet (343 metres) above sea level. It was completed in 1852 and opened by Frederick Peel who was the second son of Sir Robert, who was prime minister at the time of the Repeal of the Corn Laws and who gave his name to the Police Force first called "Peelers" and then "Bobbies". In the area around the tower there are several holes in the ground looking like small quarries. Indeed they were and the stone actually went in to construction of the tower.

These old "quarries" are ideal nesting sites for upland birds including meadow pipits and wheatears whose white rumps flash in the summer sunlight. They are common around the tower between

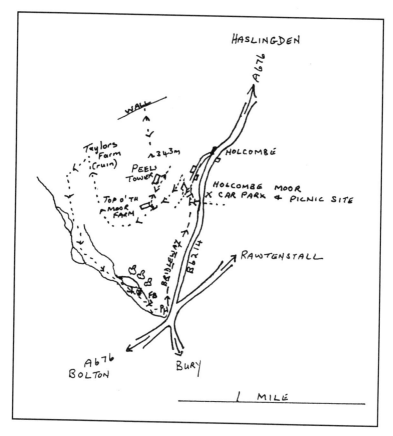

April and the end of October.

From the tower we always make a detour at right angles to the building until we reach a blind end at a stone wall. This area is another delight, with panoramic views towards Bolton and Chorley and beyond this to the coast.

Then retrace the route as far as Top O'th Moor farm. Climb a stile and keep close to the side of the farm. Continue downhill and pass the ruin of Taylor's Farm.

A feature of these upland areas is the number of rowan trees, which although native to Britain were often deliberately planted especially in the North of England. The reason was one of superstition as the red berries were thought to be a defence against witchcraft. Any new cottage or farmstead had rowan planted around it and the incomers felt safe. Rowan blossom is at its best in June and the berries are a delight in September and October. Each looks like a

19

small apple which proves that the species are closely related.

Much of the moorland around Holcombe is used by the Ministry of Defence and the Commando assault course is well known to generations of soldiers and also to those taking part in Granada TV's series "The Krypton Factor".

From Taylor's farm the route bears left and descends quite steeply and then another obvious left turn returns to the bridleway at the rear of the Hare and Hounds hotel. Rossendale had, and still as to some extent, a tradition of following the harriers in pursuit of the brown hare and the front of the hotel has seen many a stirrup cup emptied by the Master Of Hounds and so the pub is well named.

A short incline along the bridleway leads to a stile on the right hand side. Turn through this and return to the car park.

Around Hoghton Tower

Parking: The best place to start this walk is at Riley Green, and the Royal Oak hotel provides excellent food and good parking. There are, however, other places to park. Riley Green is on the right of A6061 Blackburn to Preston road. Just beyond the pub the road number changes to A675. Those approaching from Preston via Higher Walton should therefore follow the A675 which at Riley Green itself branches right to Bolton, also on the A675.

START with the Royal Oak on the right and just beyond the pub, turn right and pass an attractive group of cottages on the left. Straight in front are a couple of sturdy ladder stiles leading to a field path. Make sure that you follow the left path rather than a more obvious right track. Follow through fields and a rather pleasant area of mixed woodland. Here we have seen sparrowhawk, jay, woodpigeon, treecreeper and on one occasion we watched a pair of nuthatches displaying.

Approach and corss the drive leading up to Hoghton tower at a point close to the substantial lodge. Take time here to look down towards the A675 road where stands an impressive war memorial and up to the tower itself, one of the most interesting houses in Britain. It is open on Bank Holidays and Sunday throughout the summer and also n Saturdays during July and August. The drive which is lined with rhododendrons is an absolute treat during the early summer. It is well worth doing this walk on a day that the tower is open.

The tower is the home of the de Hoghton family who came over with William the Conqueror. The tower, which must have been impregnable, stands proudly on a hill overlooking the River Darwen. The present building was constructed mainly in the 16th century, but some of the earlier fortification remains.

It is constructed around two courtyards, the first entered from the drive and through a gatehouse tower guarding a terrace and a rose garden which delights summer visitors and is kept as a reminder of Old England. Unlike some of the more modern varieties these blooms have a strong scent.

Inside the house there is a collection of antique dolls and dolls' houses, but the tower itself has some magnificent rooms including the famous banqueting hall. It was here in 1617 that James the First was entertained and was so impressed with a bit of beef that he

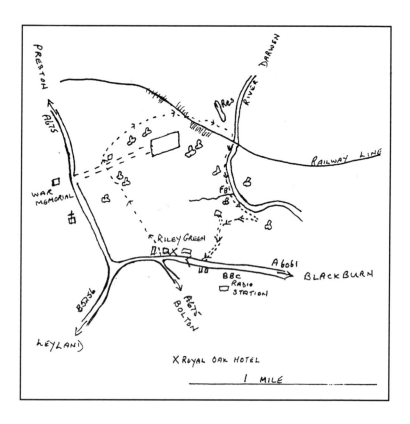

PRESTON

RIVER DARWEN

A675

Res

RAILWAY LINE

WAR MEMORIAL

FB

Riley Green

A 6061

BLACKBURN

B5256

A675 BOLTON

BBC RADIO STATION

LEYLAND)

X Royal Oak Hotel

1 MILE

knighted it and thus we have the Sirloin. It is commemorated in the name of the local pub. The table at which the King tucked into his juicy steak is still in its original place.

The walk continues by following the obvious track which goes round the back of the lodge and alongside another fine mixed woodland in which occur grey squirrels and a variety of birds. The tower is set high on the hill which looms large to the right.

Approach and cross the railway before turning sharp right parallel to the line. This meets the River Darwen, the path passing beneath the railway line and then following the river bank. The attention is drawn, especially after rain, to a weir which attracts birds such as dipper and grey wagtail although we did once have the thrill of seeing a kingfisher here in autumn of 1990. This in complete contrast to 1905 when a rambling magazine described the Darwen as a filthy river heavily polluted by effluents from the cotton mills and bleachworks around Darwen and Blackburn.

This stretch of the walk requires strong boots but, especially after rain, wellingtons are probably the best bet. There are footbridges over tiny streams running down from the sloping banks of the woodland. In spring wood anemone, golden saxifrage and celandine add splashes of colour and the area which is quiet and enclosed enough for the sound of bird song to echo clearly, even over the sound of the water.

Cross a stile and almost immediately sharp right. Do not think you are turning back on yourself but have the courage to continue onwards and upwards to a sturdy wooden gate. his area is an important spot for rearing pheasants and the birds seem to be everywhere, running quickly from hedge to hedge tails waving and legs thrashing in their haste.

Turn left on to a wide track but no not rush this section of the walk. There are thick hedges on each side and a variety of trees including alder, field maple, sloe, dog rose, oak and ash. This is a bird watcher's hedge right until it joins the A6061 at a point directly opposite the masts of the BBC radio transmitter. Turn right and follow the road back to Riley Green.

Brindle and Withnell Fold

Parking: The ancient village of Brindle is reached along the B5256 Chorley road signed Leyland off the Blackburn to Preston road (A6061). At the junction stands Brindle Bar Cottage which was the old toll house used in the 18th century during the Turnpike days. In the village there is limited parking but the Cavendish Arms has a large car park. The ale is good and the bar snacks are worth travelling miles to enjoy.

BEFORE starting off on this walk we like to spend some time enjoying the village itself. In 1990 Brindle church celebrated its 800th anniversary. Few parishes in Lancashire are older than Brindle. Although the church is now dedicated to St. James it was originally dedicated to St. Helen who was usually associated with springs or wells. It is more than likely that the village literally sprang up around a reliable source of fresh water. The first rector is listed as Ughtred in 1190, but the earliest parts of the present buildings are the tower and the Cavendish chapel which are 15th century.

The Cavendish Arms Inn was certainly in operation by 1775 and has some fine stained glass windows giving it a church-like appearance and which depict details of the Cavendish family of Holker Hall in Cumbria but who owned Brindle and were closely related to the Dukes of Devonshire.

From the Cavendish Arms, cross the road and head along Sandy Lane to the junction of Pippin street on the left. Ignore this but look carefully for a footpath on the right. Follow this past the playing fields to Marsh Lane. Turn left for a short distance to a footpath signed to the Leeds to Liverpool canal. Turn right and reach the canal at Ollerton Bridge No. 2. Descend to the towpath.

Turn right along the canal, now having your back to Marsh Lane. This leads to Withnell Fold at the canal bridge No. 88.

At the bridge turn left over the canal and continue up through the village. Note the huge mill chimney which dominates the area. Although this chimney seems to have served a cotton mill, in fact it was built to manufacture paper in 1844. This was not just any old paper, however, and was exported throughout the world for use in the printing of bank notes. Withnell Fold itself was built to provide accommodation for the workers. The site was chosen because of the presence of the Leeds to Liverpool canal which was completed in 1816 and along which could be transported coal to fuel the boiler and

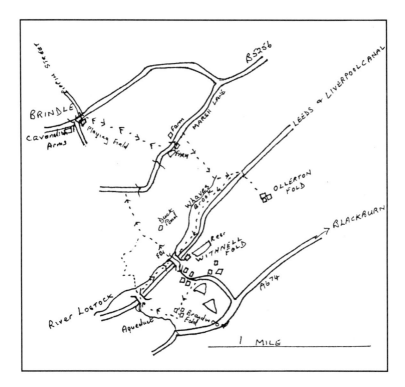

the raw materials for manufacture. The finished paper was then carried away to the markets of the world via the port of Liverpool.

The stroll up through the village reveals that the mill is now used by an engineering company, passes the memorial gardens set up to the local dead of two world wars and the Workers Reading Room built in 1890 but now a private house. Continue past the old village stocks on the left, pausing to look right to the Fold itself with its renovated cottages and the school.

Continue to follow the wide cobbled road to a point where it joins a properly surfaced road. Stop here and look right. Find a muddy track and follow it. This passes on the left one of the several lodges which once provided water for the paper mill and then the attractive little cricket field. Continue to Brandwood Fold, a solid little cluster of buildings and turn right.

Pass what is known as the aqueduct and which is a vital part of Manchester's prosperity. It is carried around 100 feet (32 metres) above the valley floor and brings water from Thirlmere in the Lake district a distance around 65 miles to the city. Continue and cross the canal to Bridge 87 and scramble down on to the canal. Return along the towpath to Bridge No. 88. Follow a wide track from the bridge above the towpath, before finding a footpath leading off left and which is not always clearly signed. The path, however, is obvious and descends to a narrow wooden bridge over the narrow river Lostock.

This area varies greatly according to the season, especially after heavy rain when the river overflows and creates an area of swamp. This is perfect summer habitat for warblers and dragonflies but also for a wide variety of flowers including water mint and meadow sweet.

From the bridge climb a flight of steep steps cut into the bank and look down left into a bird-rich area of mature woodland. Find a stile and cross it heading right. Do not continue on the footpath heading further into the wood.

Follow the path over fields but pausing to look down to the right and a small pond fringed with trees. At all times of the year this seems to be full of mallards, but there are other species of waterbirds as well so that birdwatchers are seldom disappointed. Snipe and partridge also occur, and in the spring the walk is always sure to be enlightened by singing skylarks.

The path comes out on to Marsh Lane. Turn right and continue until reaching the footpath to the left from Brindle. Then retrace the walk passing the playing fields and return to the main road turning left and this brings you back to the Cavendish Arms and a welcome drink plus a bar snack.

4 Miles

Roddlesworth Wood and Reservoirs

Parking: Adjacent to the Royal Arms Hotel is a car park next to the Roddlesworth Information Centre. The centre is open from Easter to October on Wednesdays from 1pm to 5pm, Saturdays from 12 noon to 5pm and Sundays from 11am to 6pm. It opens daily from 10am to 6pm during the local holidays. The car park, however, is always open as is the picnic site and another car park at Slipper Lowe situated a short distance beyond the Royal Arms on the road towards the Bolton road. There is also a regular 'bus service to the area from both Blackburn and Darwen. The Jubilee tower is visible from the car park and a nature trail leaflet can be obtained form the Information Centre, the Royal Arms and from a shop in nearby Tockholes village. This circular walk is based from the Information Centre but it is also possible to route it from Slipper Lowe car park and picnic site.

FROM the car park near the Royal Arms cross the road and pass through a kissing gate near which is a display board on which is a map of the area with all the footpaths marked.

The land is administered by North West Water and though walkers and their dogs are welcome, even after privatisation, it should never be forgotten that this is a drinking water catchment area. The woods consist of 185 acres with oak, ash, alder, hazel and sycamore being dominant, but there are a number of conifers present including spruce, Scots pine and larch. The latter is an example of a deciduous conifer and looks delightful in spring when the needles are a most delicate shade of green and again in autumn when they are an attractive rusty colour.

Beyond the Information Board the wide path descends to the left and the presence of cobbles suggest the presence of a lost hamlet. Halliwell Fold's ruins straddle the path and take us back to the days before the construction of the reservoirs when this was farming country. The settlement was bought by Liverpool Corporation in 1848 and was absorbed into the catchment area. The farms had specialised in providing teams of chain horses which found work in delivering coal from the small mines at Withnell to the mill at Hollinshead.

The name Halliwell suggests the presence of a holy well. To find this follow the track signed Hollinshead Hall. Initially this path climbs to Slipper Lowe car park. Here the authorities have provided a bird feeding station which is kept stocked, especially in winter, by

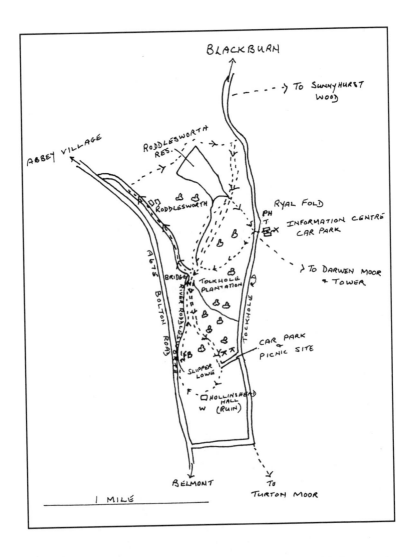

picnickers using their cars as a hide. All the common birds occur in some numbers, but rarities such as great-spotted woodpecker and nuthatches do occur and have to run the gauntlet from the attentions of magpies and the ever-aggressive grey squirrels.

From Slipper Lowe the path turns sharp right alongside the road before descending to the ruins of the once very impressive Hollingshead Hall now being restored as an impressive ruin. Here, far from being a ruin, is the Holy Well visited since medieval times by those in search of a cure for eye complaints. Nowadays visitors wonder from a distance if it is a dungeon because its windows are barred and its stout blackened oak door which is padlocked. Looking through the windows it appears to be a chapel built into the side of a hillside with Greek-like columns dripping with water. In the 18th century the structure was constructed around the well.

The hall itself and associated farms are in the process of being excavated, a project destined to go on well into the 1990s. There was a hall on the site from the 14th century but this was replaced in the 18th century by a substantial building and it is highly likely that the Well House was constructed at the same time.

Our route continues by following the wide carriage road which led to the hall and which returns to the area of Halliwell Fold where there is a bridge. We once stood on this bridge and both began to talk at the same time. There was a mist over the water and our thoughts concerned why Liverpool Corporation felt they had to get rid of the very small farming community to prevent pollution of the city's water supply.

On this walk ignore the signs to the Nature Trail, and follow the coach road to Roddlesworth. An obvious footpath leads between Roddlesworth Upper and Lower reservoirs. Ignore the upper water and follow the path alongside the lower reservoir which is fringed by trees — mainly conifers. This area is surprisingly like Scotland especially when there are anglers rowing boats on the water and woodpigeons are calling from the tops of the trees or carrying out their wing-clapping display flights over the mirror-like surface.

A right turn at the end of the reservoir leads to a steep path up to the trees to join the carriage road along which a narrow path climbs up left and back to the Royal Arms car park.

Wayoh and Turton and Entwistle Reservoirs

Parking: There are several large lay-bys just off the A666 Blackburn to Bolton road beyond Darwen. Any of these can be used as a focus for this long circular walk. There is plenty to see so do allow a whole day and if in doubt carry your lunch with you.

ON THE LEFT of the busy road leading to Bolton, opposite a plantation at which a minor road leads off to the right, find a stile. Cross this into a field and proceed keeping a drainage ditch to the left and swinging gently right with Turton Heights dominating the skyline. Follow along the top edge of a small plantation keeping a wary eye open for the sparrowhawk which is resident hereabouts, as is the goldcrest whose quiet squeaking song can be heard on windless days.

A song of a different kind is the hum of pylons as current flows along the wires. Pass beneath these after turning left towards the buildings of Spring Bank Farm. From here bear right towards Clough House Farm passing through stiles on the way towards the railway embankment at Turton Tower. As described in walk No. 10 a railway bridge has been castellated to fit in with the architecture of the Hall.

The route now meets the Chapeltown-Bromley Cross road built between 1795 and 1799 and passing close to the entrance of Turton Tower. Turn left and within a short distance a footpath strikes off past a concrete pill box built during the second world war with the threat of invasion very real and the nation determined to defend every foot. Many of these boxes have been demolished. Some effort should be made to preserve those we have left. In their own way they are as much a part of our history as Turton Tower itself.

From the pill box there is an obvious path across a field descending to Jumbles Country Park (see walk 4).

Jumbles, however, has to be passed and this is done by crossing a footbridge. Turn left and follow Bradshaw Brook through an avenue of trees emerging at a row of three old weavers' cottages. Look for a stone bridge on the left and emerge on to the cobbles of Vale Street. Find Vale House a delightful 18th century house with a horse mounting block against the wall, but a right turn leads to an even greater treat — a pack horse bridge dating to 1691. This was handloom weaving country and this was the route between Chapeltown and Affetside. Each leading horse had a set of bells which were usually made in Wigan and the jangling noise they made especially in fog

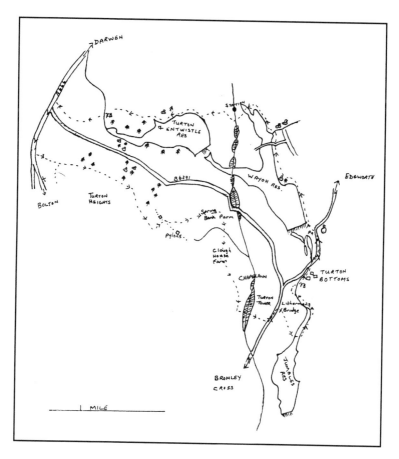

gave warning of their coming.

A little beyond the bridge is Birches road. Turn left and continue beyond yet more attractive cottages to Bolton Road. Approach the church with a pub opposite. Turn left and follow the embankment of Wayoh reservoir. This opened in 1876 to provide compensation water for Bolton. In 1962 Bolton had an increasing demand for domestic water and the reservoir was provided with a treatment works and enlarged so that it now holds 501 million gallons and is capable of treating and delivering 10 million gallons per day. There is a pleasant viewpoint area to the right of the path which is an ideal place to pause for a picnic and beyond this a number of nature conservation areas have been established.

Ignore the left turn at Crow Trees Lane leading to Entwistle Hall Lane but continue on crossing a feeder stream passing through a plantation before swinging left towards Entwistle station. Crossing the railway line just before the Strawberry Duck Inn which is rightly famous for its cuisine. There is an interesting bit of industrial archeology hereabouts in the form of a rusting iron gantry which actually spans the footpath. This once carried materials from Entwistle station to the Know Mill bleachworks which was demolished in 1958 in preparation for the enlargement of the reservoir mentioned above.

From the Strawberry Duck continue towards Turton and Entwistle reservoir and find a footpath across fields to the Hall Shores Plantation on the shores of Turton and Entwistle reservoir. Pass through Lower House Plantation and Simms Meadow Plantation. All these are excellent bird watching areas, and there are fine views of Turton Heights over the water.

At the end of Simms Meadow plantation either a left or a right turn will lead to a footbridge over Cadshaw Brook. The left fork leads along the edge of the reservoir and the right fork over fields. In any event the routes are obvious.

At the end of the Fox Hill plantation follow the wide cart track and then bear left across a couple of old stone walls. Find a plantation and follow it to a cutting known as Yarnsdale, through which rushes Cadshaw Brook on its way to the reservoir.

Look upstream to a huge outcrop known as the Fairy Battery which is now a magnet for apprentice climbers but it was once a magnet of a different kind. Until the Conventicle Act was passed in 1664 any religious service other than that prescribed by the Church of England was illegal. Non-conformists such as the Walmsley Unitarians from the Egerton area worshiped at the Battery and hoped no-one reported them.

After crossing the footbridge bear left, climb the steps cut into the hillside at the top of which is a sign erected by the Holiday Felowship. They certainly know where to erect signs as the views from here are excellent.

Follow the obvious track to meet an even wider path from an old quarry and descend to the A666 and the car parks.

Turton Tower and the Stone Circles

Parking: Turton Tower is on the bus route from Bolton to Bury (565) and Bolton to Edgeworth (563) and by car by turning off the A676 between Blackburn and Bolton onto the attractive B6391. Although there is some parking close to the Tower this has its own parking and in any event this walk should always allow ample time to explore the building which is now a museum. It is open from Saturday to Wednesday from 12 noon to 6 pm but including bank holidays.

BEFORE starting off on this walk make sure you have strong boots or Wellingtons and give yourself some time to think and set the tower in context. Prepare also for a rather tough moorland walk.

Before the industrial revolution Turton was a strong fortified tower set at the foot of rugged moorlands which are very much out in the wilds. It was built around 1400 at a time when England and Scotland were constantly at war and this area was well within reach of the border. The first owners of the estate were the Torbocs who were absorbed by the Orrell family and it was they who created a fine Tudor style house. Perhaps they spent too much money on the house because in 1628 the house passed to Humphrey Chetham a textile merchant and banker, but he did not evict the Orrels who continued to live in the hall until 1648.

By 1653 however Humphrey's nephew George Chetham lived in and loved the hall but the premature death of his son in 1659 destroyed the father's interest. After years of neglect and use as a farmhouse Turton was bought in 1835 by James Kay whose textile businesses in Preston and Manchester had made him rich and he made extensive alterations to the house. Some have said that he removed much of the character but we disagree because without Kay's expenditure the Tower would have been a ruin and may well have vanished for ever.

The Kay family left the Tower in 1890 and in 1903 Sir Lees Knowles bought it. In 1930 his widow ensured that Turton Tower was given to the local authority and Blackburn council now administer it as a museum.

Find a track close to the entrance to the Tower and on the right hand side pass a waterwheel. This has nothing to do with the Tower but was transported from a nearby mill by the local historical society in 1978. It does, however, add atmosphere to the area even if it is a little out of context.

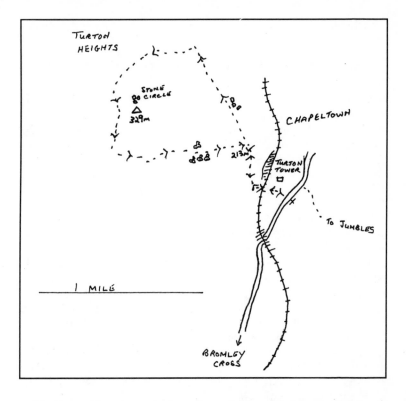

Much more in context is the railway bridge which is crossed. Look over and at the battlemented bridge. When the Bolton to Blackburn railway was opened in 1848 the Kay family gave permission for the track to cut through their grounds providing the bridges were given battlements to blend with the architecture of the tower.

From the railway bridge the path continues straight into a mixed belt of trees where early one winter's morning we saw a fox sprinting across the path leaving footprints and a mark where its brush had swept along the snow.

At a junction of paths, bear right through a gate and follow the obvious track which climbs past farms and up sloping damp fields. This is where you need waterproof shoes but the views are magnificent and provide lots of excuses to have a breather and take in the panoramic beauty.

After reaching a road continue along it for a short distance until you pass a plantation beyond which on the left is a stile. Cross the stile and skirt the fence keeping it hard on your left. The fence then winds round to the left but at this point have courage and look at the overhead electric wires leading to a prominent pylon and carry on straight past it relying on your lung power. The view is of Rivington Hill and the communication masts on Winter Hill.

The descent is not always obvious but walking straight towards the Winter Hill masts is an ideal marker and after meeting a stream, there is an embankment after which the path is once more obvious. The stream has a pair of resident dippers and we once found the nest of a grey wagtail tucked under the bank.

After following the stream for a while, head away from the bank towards a line of trees and find a gate at the bottom of the hill. An obvious path then traverses the field to a substantial stile. Much of the route so far has provided rural views but on this section the aspect becomes more urban with the sprawl of Bolton and Manchester very obvious. We try to arrange to do this walk on an autumn evening as the town lights are switched on and on one occasion we waited until dark to get the full impact of the view.

After crossing the stream keep the ridge on your left and continue for almost a mile along a gentle path with gates and stiles all kept in good order. The route then becomes enclosed by narrowing walls on either side leading to a narrow stile. The path turns left in front of a farm and then after joining a farm track turn left through an obvious gap in the wall.

It is now decision time. is it worth making a short diversion to see the stone circles? Actually it is but do not expect to see Stonehenge or something resembling Long Meg, Castlerigg or Swinside circles in Cumbria. You need to know they are there to recognise just what they are.

Having said that, press on by turning half left and climbing steeply across very wet rush-strewn pasture. Although there is no obvious path there is a Trig. point at which to aim standing 1075 feet (326 metres) above see level. There are stones around the pillar but in the 19th century well meaning vandals who called themselves antiquarians removed and rearranged the stones. This means that modern archeologists are unable to get a clear idea of what culture arranged them but they possible date to around 3,000 BC.

To return to Turton stand at the Trig. point and face Winter Hill masts. Head downhill and left until you find a very obvious path where a fence meets a wall. Pass through a gate on the left and follow the path keeping the wall on the right. Look across to Holcombe Moor and down at Chapeltown in the valley.

The route leads through a gap in a wall into a small but very attractive mixed woodland and then over a stile. The track is now broad and an obvious right return leads back to Turton Tower.

Around Turton Moor

Parking: The same car park at Slipper Lowe is used as in Walk No.8.

LEAVE the car park and follow the footpath to Hollinshead Hall as in Walk No. 8. It matters little how often this short stretch is covered for throughout the 1990s work will be going on to provide the historic site and an interest in wildlife. The footpath meets a gate on the Tockholes road, an ancient track.

Follow this to a right angled bend where it joins the A675 road linking Blackburn and Bolton. Find a stile in the left hand corner. We are usually accompanied by a well behaved black labrador but we always take notice of the sign inviting walkers to keep their pets under control. A dog running free does not have to chase sheep - pregnant ewes only have to *think* it might, to run headlong away and then they run the risk of aborting. They seem to know that a dog on a lead can do no harm. We walkers should remember that this countryside gives us pleasure, but to the farmer it is his living.

Climb the short steep path to the ruin of Higher Pasture Barn Farm from which can be seen Darwen Moor and a glance backward shows the great expanse of Anglezarke Moor. Set into the west face of the wall of the farm is a memorial stone.

Following the line of a drainage channel to yet another ruin; this time the much more historically significant Whewell's farm. During the civil wars of the 1640s with Englishmen slaughtering each other in the name of God and King or God and Parliament much innocent blood was shed. The ardent royalist the Earl of Derby attacked Bolton and after a stout resistance the townsfolk were put to the sword. With its victory Parliament sought revenge and the Earl was returned to Bolton to be executed. He was kept the night before his execution in 1651 at the Old Man and Scythe. The Inn still stands and it is said that his drinking cup and the chair in which he sat are on display and are genuine. At one time the axe which cut his head from his body was also on view, but what is known about his executioner? He was one George Whewell of Whewell's farm who set out early on the morning of 15th October to attend to his grizzly business.

After passing what is left of the farm bear right to meet the busy A666. Turn right along this for a very short distance passing a plantation on the right close to the junction of the A666 with a minor road.

Find a stile and continue up the side of the plantation and towards

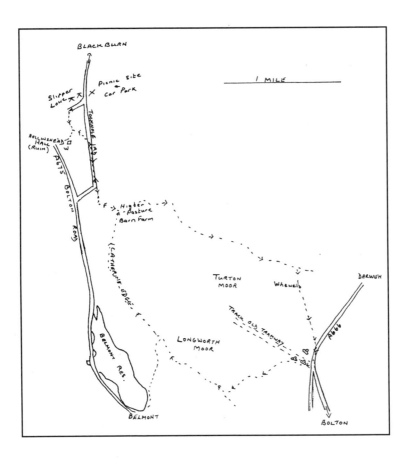

Longworth moor.

Hereabouts is what looks like part of an old railway track - it is in fact a remnant of the days of the local mines which exported their coal along an inclined tramway. Coal had been mined above Belmont for centuries and during the 19th century there were three very busy operations, the last to close being Turton Moor colliery in 1920. It is the tramway to this enterprise which can still be detected close to the plantation.

Following the path leads to a signed footpath down into the village of Belmont but this should be ignored and track followed on to Catherine Edge. Down into the valley on the left there are views of Belmont reservoir which once provided water for cotton mills and bleach works. Belmont reservoir was constructed in 1826 and as the demands for water continued as mill owners and bleachworks managers cried out for more supplies other streams were dammed to produce the Turton and Entwistle reservoir in 1838 and Wayoh in 1876.

Looking down at Belmont today, especially on a summer Sunday, it looks anything but industrial as members of the Bolton Boating Club sail across its blue waters with colourful sails billowinig in the slightest of breezes, each yacht being mirrored in the surface and followed by a creamy white wake.

Follow the obvious path to Lower Pasture Barn farm and then climb steeply back to Higher Pasture Barn farm. From here retrace your steps to the car park, but this is not at all boring especially in spring and early summer when it is a naturalist's paradise with breeding skylark, meadow pipit, wheatear, red grouse, redshank and curlew.

On one windy winter's day we spent an hour watching a short-eared owl slowly quartering the moor in search of the short-tailed field voles which thrive here and early on a September morning we watched a merlin dash across the ruins of Hollinshead Hall in pursuit of a goldfinch.

This walk reaches into history, natural history and industrial archeology. To misquote a beer commercial "Only Lancashire can do this," and we always feel restored when we walk its moorlands.

Lever Park and Rivington Pike

Parking: Rivington is signed from the A675 Blackburn to Bolton road at Belmont and from the village follow the obvious brown signs labelled Great House Barn and Information Centre. The car park is extensive and there are good facilities for the disabled. If you are in any doubt whether to pack a meal don't bother. The snack bar serves the most delicious homemade soup and the sandwiches are always fresh.

THIS ROUTE begins by walking away from the Great House barn through the children's play area (keep dogs on lead here, please). Turn sharp left and follow the line of the fence down into a clough, which is then spanned by a substantial wooden bridge. The sensitively balanced conservation work which has gone on here in the last ten years is commendable.

We once watched a jay here apparently playing with a cigarette end which a careless walker had discarded. It seemed to be rubbing the smoking tab-end into its feathers. We have seen both jays and green woodpeckers do this with ants and the experts think that it is only way of killing the lice and other parasites which get into their feathers.

Down to the right of the path, which climbs by means of steps out of the clough, there are views through a screen of trees down to Lower Rivington reservoir.

The reservoirs around Rivington are all favourite haunts of ours especially in winter when they play host to a fascinating assortment of wildfowl including whooper swans, goldeneye, tufted duck, pochard and teal. The area must be richer now in wildlife than it was before the city of Liverpool caused so much disruption here. When the port was expanding rapidly during the 19th century its existing wells and streams proved totally inadequate to satisfy its needs. Private water companies held people to ransom (could this happen again we wonder?) and the city began to look inland to the hills, traditionally areas of high rainfall. Rivington was much higher than Liverpool and the water could flow down through pipes purely by gravity.

Thomas Hawksley devised a scheme involving the construction of five reservoirs at Lower and Upper Rivington, Anglezarke, Rake Brook and Lower Roddlesworth. In 1847 an Act of Parliament got the scheme moving and despite some opposition and procrastination, Liverpool's huge holding reservoir at Prescott was receiving piped water from the Rivington reservoir system in 1857. Liverpool's thirst however, was insatiable and the High Bullough reservoir built by Chorley Corporation Waterworks in 1850 was taken over by Liverpool in 1856 although Chorley still had a claim on a proportion of the water. Upper Roddlesworth was added in 1860, and Yarrow in 1875 before the locals claimed enough was enough at Liverpool then turned its attention to North Wales.

After what must have been substantial initial environmental damage the reservoir system now looks very attractive especially in the pink flush of a winter's sunset.

With Lower Rivington seen through fringing birch and beech to the right look up to the left where the Pike and the Pigeon tower stand out clearly on the skyline, both of which are passed later during this walk.

Join a main track and at the end of this is a small car park ideal for those who are unable to walk from the Great House Barn. A magnificently strong looking castle stands dominating the car park at the end of a short but wide avenue of trees. Actually this is not a genuine castle but a folly built by William Hesketh Lever (1851–1925) who made a vast fortune from the manufacture of Sunlight soap and also from the production of margarine and he also set up MacFisheries. His wealth enabled him to build a model village of Port Sunlight on the Wirral bank of the Mersey, but he never fell out of love with his native Bolton and bought the 365 acre Rivington Park in 1899. Part of this he gave to the local people whilst building a now ruined mansion for himself and also Rivington Pike and the castle.

Actually we should not mock the castle as it is a life-sized model of Liverpool castle long since demolished to make room for the docks of the city. Historians have at least something accurate to look at.

Follow the obivious circular path around the castle and look down at the waters of the reservoir. We doubt if anyone could avoid the sensation of being close to the sea, even if the eyes drift over the water to the mighty ribbon of the M61 motorway.

Once the circle of the castle has been completed (take your time and watch the wildlife) follow the wide path to the main road through the park. Do take care, especially if you have children or a dog, as the road is both narrow and busy. After crossing the road look for a not very obvious footpath climbing steeply up towards Rivington Pike. If you miss this it is a pity but not a disaster because there are a number of better signed paths leading to the same landmark. We chose this muddy route because it is narrow, fringed by trees and is always full of birdlife and mammals for those who walk slow and talk not at all!

As with the rest of the area a great deal of on-going conservation is evident both to the park and to the Pike which stands 1200 feet (361

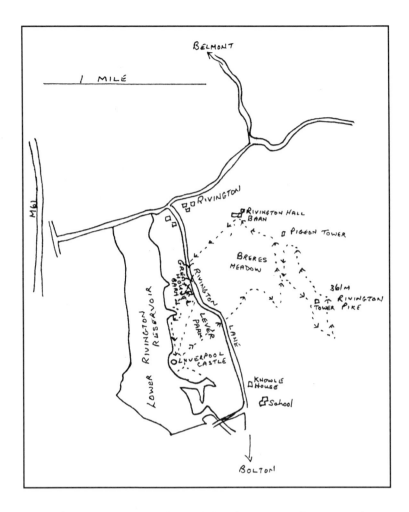

metres) above the reservoirs and the views are truly spectacular.

The obvious path is then followed in a zig-zag manner down towards the pigeon tower and the gardens which Lord Leverhulme designed between 1905 and 1921. A feature of this walk, and indeed all the local footpaths, is the provision of special stiles easily negotiated by dogs, and actually marked as such. What a refreshing change to see the companions of otherwise solitary walkers made welcome.

When Lord Leverhulme died in 1925 both the house and gardens fell into sad decay, although the park fared much better because he had left this to the local people. Liverpool Corporation bought the Leverhulme portion in 1947 and immediately demolished the house

— what a great pity! All that remains now are a few foundation stones and the Pigeon Tower.

In the recent past North West Water have encouraged volunteers to work on the restoration of the gardens and the fruits of their labours are now obvious for all to see and described in a leaflet on sale at the Information Centre.

From the gardens the route descends to Rivington Hall which was rebuilt in 1744 and is now a restaurant. Rivington Hall Barn and the Great House Barn, however, are both fine examples of Saxon "cruck barns" which are supported by huge boughs of oak.

From Rivington Hall stroll down the wide lane to the main road through the park. Cross this and return to the Great House Barn, its welcoming cafe and Information Centre overlooking the car park.

Around Upper Rivington and the village

Parking: This is the second walk which begins at the Great House Barn and Information Centre and both could be completed by the energetic with a full day to spare.

LEAVE the car park, passing close to the children's playground and follow the path keeping Lower Rivington reservoir on the left. Approach Rivington village and we always allow time to explore the church, the chapel, the village green andf the school, and there is always something new to discover.

Historians cannot give a precise date for the establishment of the church but it is certain that there was either a church or a chapel-of-ease here in Norman times. There is no patron saint, and in vierw of the fact that there is also an old chapel there can be some confusion. The mound on which the church stands is thought by some to have been a pre-Christian burial site. It is also thought that Rivington had a Christian settlement by 666 AD and the lintels over some of the windows of the present church may be Saxon. Rivington church was rebuilt by Richard Pilkington of Rivington Hall in 1540.

Rivington chapel was founded as early as 1662 by Samuel Nwton who is said to have been marched out of the church following the restoration of Charles II after Cromwell's Puritans had been overthrown. He refused to give up the religious services of the Roundheads. At first meetings which featured hell-fire sermons were held in the open but in 1702 a less oppressive attitude prevailed and a permanent building was erected. The best view of the chapel is from the stocks on the village green. Beyond the chapel is an attractive tea shop.

The splendidly unspoiled school now used by primary children was founded as a Grammar School in 1566, but the present building was erected in 1714.

After the exploration of the village follow the signed pathway to Upper Rivington and take the obvious route into the woodland. There are two alternative routes but we prefer to keep close to the water and go through Pilkington's Wood. Here we once found a mistle thrush's nest which had been constructed almost entirely from discarded crisp packets and chocolate wrapping paper. This is one way of dealing with the litter problem which despite the wardens' best endeavours can reflect the large number of people who walk around Rivington.

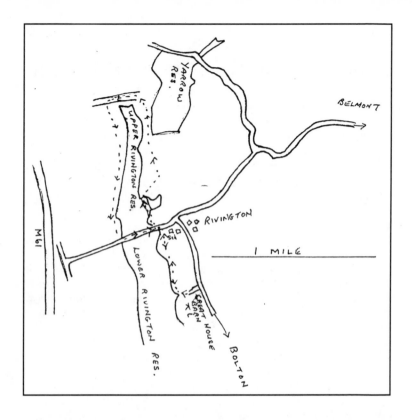

After the wood bear right and at the next junction bear left which leads to a woodland on the left and beyond this is the end section of Upper Rivington reservoir whilst to the right is the Yarrow reservoir. This complex of reservoirs constructed during the 1850s and 1860s has been supplying Liverpool with water for almost 150 years. The path approaches a junction and the left fork should be taken but it is worth going on the right fork for a short distance and then returning after finding the "Face in the Wall" — this is a carved face on a dry stone wall and is said to be a labourer's crude attempt to poke fun at his foreman.

After this amusing and worthwhile diversion return and follow the track bearing sharp left between Upper Rivington and the Anglezarke reservoir and also passing very close to the Yarrow overflow. This is often referred to as the waterfalls and although obviously artificial they are truly spectacular after a period of rain.

At the end of the track between the reservoirs turn hard left and pass Knowsley Lodge and keep woodlands on the left passing Pets

44

Grave on the right and leading to a house known as The Sreet right on the edge of the woodland. Few local houses are more impressive than the Street built in the late 19th century by a local industrialist by the name of Martin and which is magnificently set among a colourful multi-terraced garden.

Then follow a longish stretch of open path, but as it overlooks the reservoir this is bird watching country and we remember one gloriously clear day in February when it took us more than 2 hours to reach Horrobin cottage. Great crested grebes were displaying and we also watched 15 little grebes and large numbers of wildfowl including goldeneye, pochard, goosander, teal and, of course hundreds of mallards. On this memorable day, however, we watched a red throated diver, which had attracted lots of excited observers.

At Horrobin cottage turn sharp left over the narrow causeway separating the reservoirs of Upper and Lower Rivington, and return to the village. Visitors remark that the only thing Rivington lacks is a pub. This has not always been the case as a slight diversion in the village will prove. Just before the chapel pass through a kissing gate and proceed to New Hall farm and look at a gable end where you will notice a face carved in stone. This came from the Black-a-Moors Head, an inn demolished in 1903. The period of reservoir construction must have meant a roaring trade for the inn, but once the labourers had gone it must have found regular hard drinking customers hard to find. After this worthwhile diversion return to Rivington village and beyond it to the Great House Barn car park.

Lead Mines Clough, Anglezarke

Parking: There is a large picnic site and ample parking in the old Anglezarke quarry on the banks of the reservoir. Anglezarke is signed from Rivington, from Belmont and from the A674 Blackburn to Chorley road via White Coppice which itself is excellent walking country. There are no toilets but Rivington is close enough to provide facilities for all including the disabled and there is also a cafe and information centre (see walk 12). There are two walks running from the Anglezarke car parks, one out to Lead Mines Clough and a shorter woodland trail. We think this is ideal for it allows for a lunch break back at the car and saves carrying heavy food and flasks.

ALL through these walks it is so easy to forget how industrial the area once was at a time when stone was being quarried to build the mills, chapels and cobbled (or should we say setted?) streets of Lancashire in times when cotton was king. Under a clear sky it is also easy to forget the days when the run-off from the lead mines polluted the streams and killed the fish. The reservoirs now look almost as natural as the Cumbrian lakes but what chaos there must have been during their construction.

Leave the car park along the road towards Rivington which follows the banks of the Yarrow reservoir. Continue as far as Alance Bridge and just before this a track bears left and leads to a kissing gate. Once through this high limestone cliffs rise sheer to the left whilst down to the right is the feeder stream of the reservoir. On the stones in the water there are usually dippers and grey wagtails, whilst in the summertime they are joined by common sandpipers. For those interested in ferns this damp, sheltered and rocky area is a delight with hard fern, wall rue, spleenwort and lady fern all common.

Here too is a very strange sign which tells us that we are now in Lead Mines Clough and that we must not pollute the drinking water! With the modern emphasis on pollution control we know that the mines must have long since gone and all dangerous traces of the metal flushed away.

A few years ago the area was covered with tangles of bramble, willowherb and moorland grasses and only skilled industrial archeologists were able to interpret the hidden workings. What a transformation has taken place in recent years and the path crosses a footbridge and leads to an information board. On this is a map with the old lead mine workings drawn in and numbered. The various

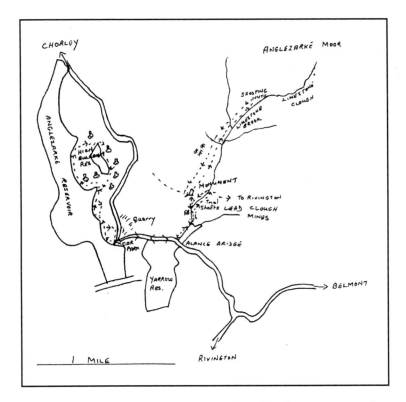

areas are then labelled on the ground or by the stream running through the clough. A leaflet may be obtained from the Information Centre of Rivington.

From the Information Board in the clough follow the lower of the two obvious paths which passes a large depression in the ground which was once the pit in which the waterwheel turned and pumped out water from the workings. The mines were worked from about 1692 until around 1840. In 1930 the dangerous shafts were filled in to provide work for the unemployed of Chorley during the depression. The main mineral mined here was lead sulphide usually called galena and this was separated from unwanted rock by crushing and washing — both very dirty processes.

The path has been routed around the labelled working areas and climbs steeply to reach a monument constructed in memory of the crew of a Wellington bomber which crashed on the moor in 1943. From this there are splendid views over to the right towards Winter hill with its communication masts standing stark like dead trees but carrying navigational lights as aircraft warnings. The crew of the

47

Wellington had no such warning during the war.

The next section of the walk requires a little care. Ignore the two ladder stiles and proceed straight ahead through a gap in the wall and then along an obvious, although usually muddy path. Follow this uphill and onto Anglezarke Moor. There have been settlements hearabouts since the Bronze Age and the time of the Scandinavian. The name derives from the name Olaf and arke meaning a hill farm, but the moors more recent use has been to provide sport for grouse shooters and there is plenty of evidence of their presence with butts discreetly positioned in the heather.

At the junction of two trails turn back on yourself and then keep a maturing conifer plantation on the right. Keep a wary eye open for sparrowhawks working their way along the moorland edge in search of unwary small birds especially meadow pipits.

The path then descends towards a broken down field wall and can be quite soft and damp at this point. Look left and see two ladder stiles. Cross either of these and you are back at the monument. After descending steps cut into the hillside by the local conservation volunteeers cross the footbridge to a small waterfall and then pass the Information Board.

The return to the car is then the reverse of the outward route, but ignore the Yarrow reservoir and look for signs of the Anglezarke quarries which seem to have provided the millstone grit for most of the streets of Manchester. Whilst working at peak the quarrymen lived in a shanty town, now gone, which had houses, shops, stables and blacksmiths for the horses, cloggers for the men and of course what must have been a lively, and probably violent pub called the Cloggers Arms.

No wonder the car park is so extensive with all this activity going on. After a break the two mile circular Anglezarke woodland trail should never be missed. The leaflet says following the red signs takes 1¼ hours but don't be mean and give yourself at least two hours. Part of this trail is also suitable for wheelchairs and viewing areas have been provided. Much good sense has gone into the planning and there is a mix of native broadleaves and alien conifers which ensures a variety of birdlife including breeding redstarts, great spotted woodpeckers and tree pipits. In winter chaffinches are always to be seen and in some harsh winters we have also seen bramblings.

This, to us, is a Lancashire walk for the next century. From the industrial dereliction of previous centuries a real rival to the natural beauty of Lakeland has been provided. It can only get better with age.